Passive Income

(How to make 100$ per day with more than 25 strategies)

Prof James Dollar

Table of content

Introduction

Chapter 1: Making a Passive Income from a small budget

Chapter 2: How to Begin with Different Strategies & Ideas

Chapter 3: How to sell Physical Products Online

Chapter 4: Membership Sites

Chapter 5: Selling Instructional Products

Conclusion

Introduction

Starting a web business and turning into financially independent is now a realistic proposition for all and sundry who has a laptop and internet access. Of the many one-of-a-kind ways to go approximately doing this, some will offer a great return to your efforts, but unfortunately many online corporations simply do no longer succeed and those operating them fail to earn enough to make it worthwhile. There are many times where a person has written an eBook and published it, or opened an online retail store, best to locate there aren't any customers The handiest manner to make cash anywhere is to have paying clients; the trick is a way to get them. There are some accurate approaches to get clients or traffic to your internet site and this book is set a success proven techniques that you can use to build a long time passive earnings from the internet.

Some of the things that worked some years ago are not feasible because the net is usually changing, growing & evolving. With 3.five billion existing customers using the net every day and another three billion potential clients in Africa, India, China and the relaxation of Asia, the sky is the restriction for new groups and an unlimited profits source. Now is the right time to catch the so known as "gravy train", but your visitors, first-class content and to be organized to do the vital work (often quite a number of work). But simply doing the paintings isn't any assure of success; you have to be operating within the right areas and doing the right matters Living from a "passive income" as it is called, is a time period now used to explain the profits human beings get hold of from the net. It is called passive profits because in theory most of the paintings is pre-finished and then you sit down again and acquire the benefits of your hard work with little work involved. In practice, any online business will require ongoing maintenance; the quantity needed relies upon at the website online, its software and the product you're supplying. There are many exceptional sorts of internet groups ranging from those that require a day by day enter to some that are totally automated.

Some net companies are sensible and sensible ways to earn cash at the net. Many humans have written some type of original highbrow property, such as an eBook, a web course, weblog posts or comparable, then installation a web save to sell their product. Whether they may be made or created by way of the operator, or acquired from other sources, there may be a considerable amount of time and power wanted to set up the website online and customize it. Once all this is finished and your website has gone stay, you'll then want to perform various advertising obligations such as selling your web page or posts and interacting with humans on social media. Finding similar websites or blogs and giving quality feedback and remarks is a great way to sell your very own web page as lengthy as it is completed in a positive way. A right weblog or internet site has fresh quality content added on a regular foundation to encourage human beings to keep coming returned, not simply pre-loaded with content and left to stagnate. Much of the material in a weblog or website can come from a person else you rent to put in writing the post for you, however you're the only who has to edit them, agenda them, and oversee the entire operation. All of these things are not passive in any respect and the profits, if any, can be very allusive in case you are not careful.

There are hundreds of get rich schemes that pop up all the time. They normally follow the identical sample or comparable rag to riches "Cinderella Story", where this man or woman was at the verge of financial ruin or committing suicide due to the fact they have been so desperate. Then, due to the affection of their family or their dog, they decided to offer the internet simply one last shot, or they stumbled across someone who, for whatever cause, gave them an immediately formulation to make fantastic amounts of money. Now they make a 6-figure earnings operating less than 1 hour each day at the same time as sitting on their non-public beach within the middle of a non-public paradise that they paid for in cash after best 1 12 months of using this system. Now they want to offer lower back and are presenting this statistics loose to you if you component with…wait for it…not $1200, or $600…or even $100. It is yours nowadays exclusively and handiest for particularly selected people at today's spot fee of $9.99, however hurry this offer is limited, (please do not trip over the huge pile of B-S).

This or some comparable such dribble will handiest make cash for the person who is promoting the scheme. If you want to take the time, and feature the capacity to create a fantasy similar to the only above, it is a reasonable way to make a passive earnings for a while, despite the fact that you need to stay with yourself knowing you are simply ripping people (commonly desperate folks who cannot find the money for it)

There is not any doubt that some human beings will make an easy dollar at the internet, but maximum people will war as a minimum at first, locating it difficult to make similar to you will in case you had a normal job. But in case you are prepared to put within the time and power wished it's far an excellent and sound manner to offer a lasting long time income. Building a solid long term passive earnings at the net requires numerous matters; the most essential is having visitors. Traffic is the term used to explain the people coming or visiting your website.

It is an easy component: the more folks who go to your site, the extra money you may make; no visitors, no money, complete stop. It does not be counted how accurate or how cheap your products or services offer is, if there is nobody to look it then no person will buy it. The 2nd very important issue is having something different humans want and is inclined to pay you to get it. The next critical aspect is your credibility on the net. This, like traffic, can make an effort to construct up, however there are several methods to speed it up. You can buy a mailing list off the internet with loads and now and again lots of e-mail addresses, however these are usually of little cost for several reasons. These lists are old and have been used by many human beings to attempt to sell their stuff so the response level may be very low.

The other cause those lists are of dubious fee is due to the fact you're better to try to get best leads of humans who've expressed an hobby in whatever you are presenting instead of simply firing emails so as to stop in maximum human being's unsolicited mail or direct mail files. If it even gets past their junk mail blockers.

This e-book will explore 30 specific strategies to creating a long time passive earnings. It will advise you of some of their properly and bad points, advantages and drawbacks, so that you can make a knowledgeable selection at the fine manner in order to proceed.

Creating passive earnings on the internet is a dream for most human beings, but it is able to grow to be a reality for every person who has a computer and internet connection. Whether you're simply starting to get interested in running on the internet and want to discover a manner to have passive profits, or when you have been suffering to make profits from it, there are some belongings you should bear in mind before jumping inside the deep quit of the net pool.

Some vital questions you should do not forget to help you decide on your best approach are:

- Do you have a product or service you want to sell? This may be a product you've got created whether bodily or intellectual.

- Do you have already got some kind of presence on the net, an internet site, weblog or social media accounts?

- Do you have a budget?

- What about your internet experience? What will you need to learn how to be a hit?

Chapter 1: Making a Passive Income from a Small Budget.

There are a few super ways to begin producing a passive earnings without spending a variety of money, however although it is feasible to run a business without spending anything, this technique would generally be a completely long procedure and require a massive quantity of paintings. The first-rate method is to establish a budget you can have enough money and work inside that. The greater amount you've got in your budget, within reason, the faster and easier it is to attain an earnings level with a view to support your lifestyle. But be conscious there are many human beings on the internet who paintings on the principle that it is simple to separate a idiot and his money so beware!

Getting a presence on the net may be done by starting on social media websites like Facebook, Google Plus, Twitter, LinkedIn, YouTube, Pinterest, and Instagram, as nicely as the use of a number of the lesser known nearby social media sites. The problem with these websites is they may be now becoming so crowded that the opposition is tough to cope with and it is straightforward on your endeavors to get lost inside the tide of statistics presented.

A few years in the past these web sites worked well. Now, with over 3.5 Billion of people's using of the internet regularly, it takes a bit to know how to apply them effectively.

Being very selective and cautious in wherein you vicinity your investment greenbacks is the key to success. To begin, you may require a web site, which might be within the shape of a general net page or probable a blog. There are many groups who provide platforms that allow you to launch and keep your website and what you pick out actually depends on what you are selling, the service you are promoting and your budget.

Web hosting web sites just like the loose Google My Sites is a great option because it has the major benefit of being unfastened, and it is easily picked up by way of the Google search engines. But unfortunately it comes with limits.

Other web sites like Blue host and Word press are my favored options. I like these websites because they're very user pleasant and have an awesome help service inclusive of a talk wherein you may talk to a business enterprise technician who can help you with any problems you can encounter. The Blue host package, for only some greenbacks a month, allows you to have a unfastened area name which include (I will use my call for an example)

www.JamesDollar.Com, so you will have your very own website. With that you can create up more than 10 sub-domain names, web pages, wherein you could sell your products or services on.

If you re promoting a cookbook for example, (whether you are the writer or just selling another author's work) your sub-area will be Organic Cooking with JamesDollar.Com The domain also comes with numerous email accounts. These are very handy and may be tailor-made to match any application which include James@James-Dollar.Com or James Cookbook@James-Dollar.Com It is constantly an excellent idea to use your name to your website. This is because there may be no doubt about whom the web page belongs to and those will accomplice your name speedy with a first-rate product. That is assuming you most effective have exceptional merchandise. If you use inferior products and do not give value for money and time spent then you'll have a very short future on the net.

If you have a product that you need to try, however without your call associated with it, you can nonetheless use certainly one of your sub-domains or create a new one by using just no longer which include your name within the internet address for that web page. For example, you can discover a brilliant choice of chef's knives and make an association with the producer or dealer to sell them, so that you can use one of your free sub- domains to do this. Another alternative is you can want to create every other eBook which includes a dessert cookbook, and that might be on a sub-area page of your most important website online, but with its own stand-alone web presence, connected or unlinked to your primary site.

When you begin or be a part of Blue host and Word press or any of the other web hosting organizations, they offer full directions on a way to installation your very own net internet site and business, at the side of a load of useful advice, so this book might not move into these physical details.

Almost absolutely passive net earnings might be carried out by outsourcing all the important work and handiest overseeing the operation, however that still requires a few input, so there is no such factor as a very passive income website. Having stated that, it's miles viable, and very reasonable, to have a really low maintenance earnings website, particularly in case you use and learn some of the tools and methods to be had from your Word Press web site in which it's miles feasible to build monetization into your Word Press site and increase the earning potential of your websites with minimal effort. To make the maximum of these websites, you will nonetheless want to do all the overall day to day web page preservation tasks which include writing new posts, marketing, and location maintenance, but the money-making method you take can be quite simple and require little paintings on your element once installation.

Chapter 2: How to Begin with Different Strategies & Ideas

When investing in any cash making enterprise, continually recall that the entirety is relative; the quantity you may count on to earn is relative to the hazard worried . A low hazard usually manner ther is a low interest price and a excessive interest price often way there is a greatly increased risk of now not most effective earning, but of also losing your investment. The quality way to determine if something can be a profitable passive earnings flow is by comparing the probably go back with the current chance-free price of return on, say, authorities bonds. The 10-year government bank bond yield is at approximately 3%, so that any challenge you try need to have a substantially better return than this, in any other case you are wasting your efforts since you may earn 3% doing nothing.

It must be noted that special countries' governments set exceptional quotes. For example, in the Philippines you may get a go back after tax (the authorities withholds the tax) of at the least 7% on authorities bonds, and those fees are guaranteed by the Philippine government. (Some might say that is a chunk risky; however they have never defaulted and are a better threat than many European countries' governments and banks.) So I would propose that if you will now not make a return of appreciably over 7% p.A. Then leave it on my own unless you're doing this for a hobby.

Internet Share Market Investing Most of us have heard how a few human beings make a huge fortune making an investment on the inventory marketplace, and indeed, you may make sizable financial gains making an investment in shares and stocks. There are some very commonplace errors that first time buyers need to be privy to before they are trying investing in shares. If you have a few hundred dollars to spare and just want to see what happens, that's ok, but if you are serious approximately creating a pleasant passive earnings, it is a real mastering curve like something else.

Don't simply bounce in headfirst, although the fundamentals of finance are quite easy in theory, that is, obtain low and sell excessive. Most humans don't, in observe, however, perceive what low and excessive truly mean. What's high to an individual World Health Organization is promoting is often taken into thought low (or low sufficient) to the buyer in any group action, in order that distinct conclusions may be drawn from the equal knowledge. Attributable to the relative nature of the marketplace, it's crucial to require your time to watch what stocks or stocks do before jumping in.

Before beginning you wish to be told as a minimum the essential metrics equivalent to e-book price, divided yield, value financial gain ratios and then forth. Perceive however they will be calculated, wherever their principal weaknesses lie and where those metrics have generally been for any inventory and its enterprise over time.

When you pop out it's so much terribly useful to use digital money in a very stock machine or with a demo account as this may assist you to acknowledge however things paintings and save a life-size add of cash to begin with.

When you initial check up on penny stocks they seem sort of a extraordinarily sensible plan. With as very little as

$one hundred, you'll get loads a lot of shares in penny stocks than you may if shopping for a blue chip inventory that might price

$50 or additional (a few a lot of more) for a share. Penny inventory provides associate degree awing financial gain if it goes up by a greenback. But, sadly, what penny shares give of their profit needs to be measured towards the volatility they need. they're observed as penny stocks for a reason; normally they are low superior organizations that, bigger usually than no longer, can no longer exercise session as a profitable deal, losing fifty cents on a penny inventory might imply a 1 hundred% loss. Losing fifty cents on a $50 deal isn't thus horrific and may usually be saved later, given time. Obtaining solid records on penny shares can even be tough, creating them a poor preference for associate degree capitalist who's still learning as they will be comparatively vulnerable. Overall, it's an outstanding plan to consider stocks in percentages and not whole buck amounts. once you initial begin out or until you become practiced in addressing stocks, it's so much high-quality for many folks to terribly own and traumatize satisfactory stock as an extended term proposition in preference to wanting to form a fast buck on low- fine businesses, as most returns on penny stocks are a be counted of success.

Do not be tempted to form investments the total factor in one precise funding; usually it's not a terrific move. Any company, even the exceptional ones, will have problems and see their stocks decline dramatically. This transpires at intervals the last financial crash. particularly while merely starting out, it's so much a thousand plan to shop for handiest a couple of shares so you're less probably to own a huge loss within the event of issues, and traditional ups and downs got to even bent expose an inexpensive financial gain. The coaching learned whereas doing this then end up to is a lot of less expensive, however still valuable.

Be terribly cautious or so borrowing to create investments as nothing is ever a particular bet. If you borrow for stocks it's so much referred to as leverage your cash. This magnifies each the gains and therefore the losses on a given funding. If you've got $100 to take a position and verify to borrow $50 to buy $150 of a positive inventory and therefore the stock rises 10%, you create $15, or a 15% come on your capital. But, on the other hand, if the stock declines 10%, you'll lose $15, or a 15% loss, however what's vital to apprehend is that if the inventory goes up by 50%, you'll build a 75% return that is outstanding, however, if the inventory declines 50%, you lose all the money you borrowed and a lot of. thus until you've got got get pleasure from it's miles wise to not borrow to create investments.

It is crucial to bear in mind that you simply might doubtless lose all of your investments over night, thus it's so much essential to only use cash you'll afford to lose. If you begin off with associate degree initial funding and build some gains, take a p.c from the financial gain and reinvest that. Then, by means that of slowly build up your total investment you may be in a very stronger perform while not risking an excessive amount of. finance ought to be viewed as a long-time amount business, whether or not or not you're a merchandiser, or a buying and holding kind capitalist. to remain in business, you wish to possess some money reserves on the aspect for emergencies and opportunities. This money can no longer earn any return, however having all of your money within the marketplace could be a hazard that even skilled patrons may not take. If you are doing not have enough money to take a position associate degreed preserve some for an emergency coins reserve, then you're no longer in a very role financially wherever finance makes sense.

Sound recommendation is difficult to get and searching to bet following huge issue or quickest growing share rate, warm tips, or engaged on rumors isn't continually a sound business set up and should be jam-packed with risks for initial time patrons. Remember, you're competitive with knowledgeable corporations that no longer best get knowledge the second it'll become accessible, however have had years of get pleasure from and recognise a way to properly analyze it quickly. If you're lucky, you'll win some, but just in case your luck runs out you'll lose everything. The exceptional coverage for beginners is to stay with investments in teams you perceive and have personal get pleasure from managing. you ought to now not affect finance like enjoying the keno. after you are severally shopping for shares among the market, you're competitive against huge mutual budget and knowledgeable patrons that try this complete-time and with a ways in which additional resources and in-depth statistics than the common person will get. after you initial begin creating associate degree investment, it's miles high-quality to begin tiny and take the hazards with money you're ready to lose, as the market may be unforgiving to any errors. As you grow to be better at evaluating shares, you may begin creating larger investments.

Money commerce exchange Forex commerce the Forex market shopping for and commerce is all or so the speculation on the speed of one country's foreign cash towards another. Being a Forex market merchandiser offers one in all the foremost exceptional capability lifestyles of any profession within the world, but it's conjointly one in all the riskiest. however if you're determined and disciplined, you can build it happen.The means it works is just in case you're thinking that the monetary unit goes to rise towards the U.S. dollar, you may purchase the EURUSD forex combine low then (hopefully) sell it at a better value to create a financial gain. If you get the monetary unit towards the buck (EURUSD), and the U.S. buck strengthens, you'll then be in a very dropping performing. Thus it's essential to bear in mind concerning the danger concerned in shopping for and commerce in Forex, and no longer only the praise. As a merchandiser you'll build a range {of money of money} fast or lose quite a few cash speedy. The terribly important issue when dealing among the money market is to know precisely what you're doing and frequently understand the precise greenback amount you've got at likelihood before moving into a trade and be all happy with losing that quantity of money, as a result of somebody exchange are a loser.

Forex is that the largest marketplace within the world, with day by day volumes extraordinary $three trillion in step with day. Anyone will open a commerce account with as very little as $250 at several retail brokers and begin shopping for and commerce a similar day in most cases. Straight through order execution permits you to vary on the press of a mouse.

it's a bonus over shopping for and commerce in shares in this there are fewer foreign cash pairs to attention on and you'll trade anyplace within the globe with the most convenient necessities being a portable computer and net affiliation. There's commission-unfastened commerce with several retail market-makers and commonplace decrease dealings prices than shares and commodities. On prime of all that, investors have civil rights to financial gain in rising or falling markets.

All novices got to bear in mind that purchasing and commerce incorporates every the capability for praise and risk.

Many of us acquire the markets thinking only concerning the praise and ignoring the hazards involved which is that the quickest manner to lose all of your commerce account money. If you wish to induce started shopping for and commerce within the forex market, get on the right music and have a glance at it initial. There are some correct sites on World Wide Web that offer unfastened courses and it's very important that you're aware of and receive the very fact that you simply will lose on any given exchange.

Chapter 3: How to sell Physical Products Online

Online Advertising

Online advertising and selling is one among the only approaches to earn cash on cyberspace. this is often notably true once you have however to earn your 1st passive on-line financial gain. however albeit it's a simple idea, in apply it's not essentially clean while not you doing right studies and mastering the good techniques to suit your man or lady application. to create an honest earnings with this sort of advertising, it needs a number of web site guests via your website thanks to the little quantity gained with the help of every click on or traveler.

Some of the good ways that to possess on line advertising and selling to your web site on-line or weblog are by approach of the utilization of the following:

AdSense

With Google AdSense you'll earn passive on-line earnings from your web site by means that of displaying ads that are applicable to your website online and its guests. one among the excellent things or so AdSense is that Google will most of the onerous paintings for

you; they notice the advertisers, decide the commercials, track the clicks, or perhaps deposit the earnings straight to your institution account each and every month. No marvel that 65% of the highest two hundred websites that show advertisements use AdSense.

Media.Net

Media.internet is incredibly like AdSense. it's the Yahoo! Bing Network's answer to AdSense ads and could be the second biggest discourse advertising and selling organization inside the globe. they need Associate in Nursing approval method that's a touch a lot of immense than

Google AdSense and need a positive range of page views month-to-month to urge Associate in Nursing account with them, however as before long as established they will give an earnings flow into this is often terribly rather like AdSense.

Chitika

Chitika is way like AdSense and Media.internet; they'll be one among the notable chance ad networks to AdSense and have an occasional minimum payout threshold. particularly if you've got a weblog with less guests, Chitika may be a premium ad network which is able to show quality relevant ads. If you've got a impressive weblog, you'll assume a impressive financial gain from Chitika.

Affiliate selling

Affiliate web advertising has been around nearly as long because the net which is one among the good and best ways to earn some positively passive profits. Affiliate advertising within reason straightforward. You earn cash on-line with the help of merchandising the merchandise or services of another leader for a fee this is often paid on each sale you create.

The normal approach is to associate up With affiliate programs and the majority major web organizations and businesses have associate advertising and selling packages. Once you be a part of and obtain their associate links, you'll begin promoting them all over, on all of your web activities In order to construct an everyday and growing long run steady earnings ensue affiliate advertising, you would like to possess traffic and to be promoting merchandise that provide folks true price. To lure humans to shop for that merchandise, you would like to possess a web site that attracts a large quantity of folks and build a trusting relationship along with your audience.

Build your own email subscriber listing from of us that head to your web site employing a service like aweber to capture emails and reply to queries. could} then be able to produce a list of humans that take into account you and need to listen to about what you've have to be compelled to say and that they may then be a lot of willing to besides your associate product recommendations.

Usually it's miles nice to limit the kinds of merchandise to those which could be closely

related to the theme or material of your web site or web log, because of the actual fact if you've got too several adverts men can shortly prove to be irritated or distracted and transfer off, associate awful heap an equivalent means we tend to do while the advertisements come back on out TV. a number of the nice affiliate broker offerings are Google Adsense , Amazon Associates , ClickBank , Commission Junction, Flex Offers, etc. all of them have numerous totally different product all told types of thoughts and niches, therefore you will make sure to seek out some quality merchandise to choose out from.

Email selling

To achieve success with email advertising it's terribly necessary no longer to be visible as a cheat or to be swamping individuals with beside the purpose direct mail. you may confirm to lose humans quick out of your mailing listing just in case you are doing. If achieved effectively and tastily although, this can be a totally successful technique of promoting because of the actual fact you're causation to those that recognize you and are receptive to you and your niche, thereby growing the chances of additional purchases.

Niche Websites

Niche websites are legitimate and successful thanks to build an excellent financial gain once you have a forte product or carrier. they'll be dedicated to 1 challenge or a locality of an issue and that they then emerge as of hobby to a select type of men, however people WHO are a lot of possible to get because of the actual fact they'll have an interest by the challenge of your web site. These sorts of websites or niche websites are a lot of simpler to place it on the market and are higher for being picked up with the help of search engines like Google, surrendering you forthwith to the proper customers.

Another way to form money from niche sites is to sell them by means that of auction at websites like Flippa. There's not any reason now not to possess an entire portfolio of niche sites; these may be of connected subjects or fully totally different impartial standalone subjects, all causative in your passive profits. once you study most successful net entrepreneurs, they personal or develop multiple websites because of the actual fact with every web site it'll increase the potential you've got for creating larger and a lot of profits.

Writing do work

People WHO are sensible at writing or who enjoy writing articles, blogs, and fast fictional tales or simply like writing in wellknown regarding nearly any topic will frequently realize there is also a marketplace for readymade, correct high-quality content that they'll be capable of promote on sites like Upwork, eLance or Freelancer. Some common sites like eHow, About.Com, and Yahoo are looking for writers and by means of promoting or even merely causative typically to those sites it may assist increase your name.

This, in turn can assist you to barter for higher and better rates furthermore as having the ability to contend for a few of the upper paying freelance jobs. Several of those can pay $50 in step with hour or a lot of. however if doing this kind of paintings, it's way vital to carry in reality with the individuals you agreement for as they like to know what's happening and to not be unbroken within the dark as a result of they typically have cut-off dates to satisfy. this can be significantly important if you've got an extended term settlement or a long term project. By causation those every-day updates you may build humans self-assurance in your competencies and asking queries insures you've got a really sensible power of the work needed.

If you ever have a method and are locating it troublesome to deliver the secure paintings or to finish your agreement, bit the individuals you're running for as shortly as potential and permit them acknowledge. Business is industrial enterprise and customary courtesy goes an extended means. Individuals got to confirm you may be trustworthy or they'll not rent you once more and should terribly effortlessly ruin your name, therefore don't ever do no matter this can be getting to hurt your name.

Search Engine improvement or computer program optimization Those men WHO have an operative power or so or fully everybody who takes the time to seek out about search engine optimization, that's however search engines or websites paintings, would find there's a giant demand for various types of articles which could be written during a fashion that optimizes get engine words inclusive of keywords, key-word synonyms, name tags, headers, bullets, etc.

Promoting Clickbank merchandise

Clickbank is now probable the most important digital products market on-line. One of the measurers it uses is called 'gravity' to represent how nicely a product sells, based on what number of sales were made and how latest the ones profits were. Clickbank has an affiliate program where you could locate a massive type of merchandise. Once you be part of up you may promote any of your very own or other human beings's products, as properly as discover folks that will sell your merchandise, so you can likely get a big following on your site.

Promoting Amazon Products

The Amazon associate program is a surely top manner to promote bodily merchandise, both your personal or other humans', via a reliable, trustworthy, and nicely- recognized on-line store. Their commissions are quite small, however due to the reality everybody is aware of Amazon they have a large amount of traffic. You can earn a commission while you ship a person to Amazon if they buy some issue else on Amazon inside 24 hours, whether they arrive to be searching for the product you promoted or no longer. So, for example, if you promoted a e-book and the person you dispatched to Amazon ended up searching for something else you will get the price for both. This can add up to a pleasing more bonus.

Promoting Commission Junction Products

Commission Junction is one of the oldest and largest associate networks on the internet today. Most in their traders are well set up which may be a bonus in case you're looking to promote larger brands. They provide several options which incorporates pay in keeping with sale offers, pay steady with lead offers and other styles of offers.

Promoting DigiResults Products Online agency and net advertising merchandise are the principle matters DigiResults recognition on, however they also have other products ranging from fitness and health to journey. Vendors and affiliates receives a commission at the point of sale, and no longer a month or later like most affiliate marketplaces, which makes them extra attractive.

Simple Virtual Assistant Jobs

Although this is not strictly passive earnings as you need to hooked up a small quantity of effort, these things are right due to the reality you gets a fee for doing (very) clean tasks on line.

Cashbacks

This is a great way to get rewarded for buying or the use of products you plan to shop for anyway. Cashback net web sites pay you at the same time as you click on through them, pass to retailers, and spend. There are nicely over 2,000 shops that provide cashbacks together with Walmart, Target, Sears, Calvin Klein, and others. You can also get a $10 gift card after your first $25 well worth of purchases. Sign up is free.

Taking Surveys

There are many loose survey web sites providing customers the capacity to gets a fee for taking surveys on-line. These web sites must all be loose and if you come upon a survey net page where signal up isn't loose, clearly avoid it. There are too many fantastic websites.

Take a test Global Test Market, Mobrog or Toluna Survey Center. You will never get wealthy taking surveys, but it is an interesting manner to spend a few idle minutes and pay for that atypical coffee.

Answering Questions

There are so many people asking questions on line and in case you're an expert on your field, you can generate profits through answering those questions. JustAnswer.Com is a business enterprise that lets in you to sign up for their crew of specialists and serve a patron base of extra than 20 million people. Fightfox.Com is a place for journey specialists so check them out. They have tremendous reviews and nice commentary quite an lousy lot everywhere.

Writing Reviews

There are many corporations so as to pay you for writing reviews of their merchandise and offerings, mainly if you have a properly-installation blog or other on-line presence this is in the identical or a comparable field.

Target Your Own Advertisers

There isn't any cause why you cannot goal advertisers directly who've or are marketing products relevant to your content material and offer them offers or an association to promote your products and you to promote theirs.

Selling eBooks

If performed the right way, selling eBooks may be quite an exceptional passive income stream. Once you have got posted your e-book and it's miles there permanently, it will clearly preserve on promoting a few copies (or if you're lucky, loads of copies) for years to return. Because there are thousands and thousands of books out there, it's far regularly difficult to break into this market and it does take time to put in writing a good e book and generally it will take some time for it to start selling and offer you with an earnings, however in case you've got masses of expertise about a particular subject matter and prefer to jot down, the new generation makes it without a doubt easy for every body to jot down, edit, and self-put up your own eBook for free. With little problem you could make a fantastic income with eBooks. You can sell it for a little price like $0.99, all of the manner up to +$100, relying on the content and the decision for books of your chosen topic.

One of the clearly exquisite subjects approximately writing and self-publishing eBooks is that most of the on line e-book stores which consist of Amazon, (who're by manner of a long way the maximum important) further to nearly all the others, will listing and sell it for you with no in advance fees. You pay a commission on income and that they deal with everything, including marketing sales and ebook distribution, then deposit the money into your account or send you a take a look at. You are also free (as you own the e e-book) to sell and promote

Selling your eBook on Amazon

If you're aiming to promote eBooks, then Amazon is that the wonderful preference thanks to the actual fact they're the most important on-line eBook distributor and generate around 3 quarters of all eBook sales through their web site. they're going to give you with a return of 70% royalty on every e-book sold . the simplest drawback is that they are doing no longer reveal the e-mail address of the customer so you can't transfer them on your mailing listing for updates and future financial gain

Swing your eBook on Your Own web site Having your own website, and mercantilism your terribly own and alternative humans books and merchandise could also be very moneymaking. You gain the eye of your customers and also the capability to feature them to your list so you'll be able to invite them to come back on your web site therefore you can give them some a lot of your merchandise or services.

This is a part of constructing up the all- necessary web site guests, specifically this kind of tourists as those folks have already come back to you in order that they are a lot of doubtless to emerge as repeat or traditional customers; this can be what's thought to be fine visitors.

Online Courses

If you may write Associate in nursing eBook there could also be no reason you can't write or produce an online path. This can be another excellent thanks to leverage it slow and energy with the help of teaching some factor once and obtaining bought it once more and again. Many of us sense that an online path or categories are bigger valuable than eBooks, primarily thanks to the actual fact they'll give transmission content material comprehensive of video and audio and not merely text. They generally additionally supply support, steering or education as a region of your direction that adds even further worth.

There isn't any reason that each person needs to be restricted to promoting digital product. Selling or reselling physical merchandise is also terribly profitable. Creating a living by getting wholesale and reselling on this on-line marketplace places has ne'er been easier.

EBay

e-Bay is currently the foremost vital and most well- renowned auction and buying electronic computer out on internet, with every country having its personal native chapter additionally to the first international web site on-line. the worth varies from usa to u. s. and customarily you pay a little insertion value to listing your product & a little a part of the price (10%) once your item sells. Often, they run distinctive promoting offers and at the instant, the insertion costs for your initial fifty listings in step with period of time are free. You'll additionally open an eBay save just in case you would like to sell on a standard basis. There are some excellent profits to be created via buying merchandise which might be low cost and marketed poorly or with laws that you simply should purchase and re promote beautifully at a terrific markup.

Re-Selling different People's Stuff on eBay

Sometimes you may find things during which the oldsters United Nations agency listed them weren't terribly careful close to however they indexed them, while not an image, terrible descriptions, no reserve, and different limitations that have stopped folks shopping for. These will prove to be a true good buy for the clever capitalist. By buying these gadgets on the correct bargain value, then advertising them well with right photos and descriptions, it's possible to sell them at an enormous earnings for nearly no effort. Another properly plan is to push things on behalf of people United Nations agency, for no matter cause, don't wish to push it themselves.

You only comply with take a reciprocally prearranged fee.Checking out church fairs, garage sales, vintage fairs, estate sales, chance outlets, and auction homes, you may often notice all manners of stuff being sold-out at a discount price. These sorts of things will bring sensible sale on eBay (or each different comparable website). When just some clean sales, you may doubtlessly double or quadruple your money.

Drop Shipping

Drop transport is that the closing passive profits supplier. it should be created to be undoubtedly machine-controlled along with your handiest input being to visualize the system and coins the checks. The term drop shipping is once you produce a store the front that offers product from sure makers. The client visits your save, orders a product, or locations AN order with you, & someone else (usually an assembly commercialism in the other U.S. of a, often Asian country, or somewhere in South East Asia) makes the merchandise inexpensively and ships it without delay to the patron. You don't ship the money to the manufacturer till when the consumer has paid you, therefore there's no threat concerned, you ne'er even see, handle, or do one thing with the bodily product excluding management the complete method (and even that will be outsourced just in case you actually need).

As a vendor, that's very economical because of the actual fact you don't ought to have any inventory, overhead prices, storage prices, and tiny or no liability. Therefore once you have a decent conception for a product that may be industrially created at an inexpensive value, it may be

Unique or some issue somebody else provides, and then drop shipping is maybe a first-rate chance for you.

Once you've got a product, by means that of the usage of the drop ship technique, you may promote anyplace, additionally to in your own keep, the employment of companies like eBay or Amazon, or a number of the choice internet sites that are cited during this chapter to achieve the widest audience possible.

Take a look through Amazon in the slightest degree the products on the market. The name makers are all there with their huge mark ups (you get hold of the name, not invariably the quality) and every one the look-alike merchandise are there additionally. several of them are poorly diagrammatical, therefore if your chosen product is given nicely, your SEO is in situ, and you've got priced it to vie, there's immeasurable money to be crafted from the three.5 billion individuals the usage of the net.

Craigslist

Craigslist does no longer provide the same functions as eBay but it's loose and plenty of humans find that it's far less tough and quicker to use. You do no longer have to be part of to end up a member, no matter the fact that that is an choice in case you need to be able to keep music of your posts and repost your products.

Etsy

Etsy is a chunk like eBay, but is focused on in general handmade or antique products. Perfect if you're selling something artsy and crafty as they have got an annual turnover in extra of two billion greenbacks and so are famous.

Shopify

Shopify is very simple and smooth to set up. It provides alternatives as a way to build your very personal e-commerce save from scratch. It has an smooth to apply admin interface with over a hundred cellular responsive topics and masses of high-quality add-on apps for all of your e-trade desires.

Weebly

Weebly is a smooth and affordable way t assemble your very own internet website as well as a web save or blog. You can pick out your very personal or use one of their many problem matters, placed your web web page together the usage of a available drag- and-drop creator, download the cell app and start running a blog and selling immediately away. It is likewise a splendid website on-line to apply to manipulate your advert and promoting campaigns, manage social media channels and craft stunning newsletters.

Simplesite.Com

This website gives you a unfastened website which incorporates a private domain, precise designs, amazing consumer service, as well as being cell and pill optimized,

Seek engine advertising optimized and is derived with your private unfastened online keep. It's the perfect way to start a web passive income commercial enterprise on a shoe-string budget.

Selling Other Digital Products

There are many different kinds of virtual merchandise you can sell, in fact, whatever you can do not forget has a ability market with 3.five billion humans on the net.

Selling the Websites & Domain Names like Flippa.Com is a fantastic internet site on line for getting and promoting web websites and domain names and similar to many things, such as real property, those can circulate up in cost over time. Often, if you don't forget a extraordinary domain name and it is not taken, you could promote it. If someone wishes that call it can be well worth loads and domain names sell from approximately $10 upwards, with some of the more popular ones fetching numerous thousand. In fact, sometimes a really terrific domain name can be well worth many thousands of bucks. Think coca-cola.Com or gottahaveacoke.Com. This may take a piece of time and knowhow however need to produce pleasing Passive earnings over time.

Sell Photos

If you've got an extraordinary camera and prefer taking pix, internet websites like Shutter stock and Graphic Stock will accept a wide variety of superb images and then promotes them on their sites for a royalty rate. This can provide you with a splendid steady circulate of passive profits, as they all have loads of hundreds of traffic daily. These are the web sites many companies use to effortlessly and conveniently find out the photographs they use for their websites and merchandise. The track which you hear even as the company you call is busy and you're located on keep, even as listening to advertisements, or pay attention while looking a promotional video or something on you tube, frequently come from groups who promote stock music inside the same manner as they promote photographs and other snap shots. If you're musically inclined, there may be coins to be made with the useful resource of recording yourself. There is a regular call for as human beings look for fresh precise expertise and you do now not should be an expert to make money at this.

For those human beings who really like photography or recording yourself or friends gambling an instrument, don't allow those images visit waste even as you could without troubles license them thru a royalty free internet site that specializes in inventory snap shots or music. Each time a person uses a few thing you have licensed you can collect a small charge or price that, over time, ought to construct into a pleasing little income pass to add to all of the other profits streams you ought to be creating.

Chapter 4: Membership Sites

Many websites now have an area this is protected via a membership-only portion. This is a very good idea because it means you can have free site visitors that you can attract with an array of interesting and valued objects and then endorse to them that they could get the full advantages of your website and save cash by means of joining for a nominal fee. This can be a very powerful manner to generate online earnings and perform a service-based enterprise. If you have got your individuals paying a month-to-month or yearly fee

to get access to a password-blanketed location where unique content is made available and you offer remarkable value and a broad interest base (or a specialized niche) to hold your clients happy as well as trying to spread your commercial enterprise by means of phrase of mouth to others (considered one of the most productive strategies of building a web enterprise), you may transform a mean site into a totally worthwhile recurring income- generating business, bringing a normal go with the flow of income from the equal purchaser base.

One of the other benefits of a club website online is that you can begin your site or release it without it being absolutely complete. In fact, through simplest creating a small part of your real content, you could allow it to develop organically with content from your customers. This can be a big benefit and you're getting paid in advance. This offers you the advantage of having a website that has content material that human beings absolutely want, you get quality, actual time feedback, which helps you to provide and make sure that you are growing a product or service based totally website online

this is imparting contents that your customers want, and not just a website that has stuff that you assume or wish they might want.

Often people will spend a variety of time, power and money growing a first-rate website online that no one definitely wishes and so nobody can pay for. The secrets of internet marketing are to offer relevant information that people need in an smooth to find and recognize format and at a realistic low cost price, but it must be user friendly and simple. The simpler the better as humans will no longer bother in case you complicate matters.

Selling Software

Selling software program can be one in all the most lucrative passive income streams you could try. Many human beings do no longer think of it because they do no longer have the revel in or the technical capabilities inclusive of programming, or the different sorts of software program writing abilities, but this aspect isn't important. The reason is because all of this will be carried out through other humans who you could discover at the net without a lot difficulty. Once you discover a good application developer and feature a good concept, (this is the important part), it becomes smooth. If you can discover a small, however very useful service or product in an area that needs to be addressed and provide an answer for what's needed, the software you develop does no longer need to be high-priced or feature-wealthy to be successful. Often a small device that solves a huge need, if priced right, can be very profitable, getting again to those 3.five billion people (plus an expected additional 3 billion over the following couple of years) on the net. If you could get $1 from 0.001% of these people you could be getting a go back of $35,000 and if you could make that a recurring charge it turns into very profitable.

Website Services

Nowadays absolutely everyone is starting an internet site or webpage, whether it's the usage of a home desktop PC, a laptop, or a hand held device, maximum human beings are not technically savvy. In fact, most are technically challenged. When putting in place a internet site or page there are a hundred and one things to do, which include all types of putting in, programming, and small tricks to know if you need matters to appearance perfect. Most human beings cannot be troubled and would be inclined to pay a person to do it for them. If you've got any talent at putting in websites and anything associated with internet site introduction including SEO, post writing, growing graphics, developing internet site themes, programming, etc, then you may easily promote your offerings to humans who want them. Places to find these humans are Upwork, Freelancer, or some of the other digital assistance sites. The People also look out at Facebook, eBay

Chapter 5: Selling Instructional Products

At the moment, the fastest growing location on the internet, both for locating matters and having a web presence, is Instagram. It is so easy and effective it has taken over Facebook and YouTube due to the huge amount of garbage they have each now collected.

Right now the biggest Instagram customers are girls over forty five years antique and this is no joke. It used to be teens on

Facebook, however because of the new smart phones, these often technically challenged users have become the biggest users and also the most important spenders with an anticipated user price of 45%, and with their relatively big spending budget, these humans are normally at the degree of existence after they have a touch spending electricity and are happy to apply it.

If you can write an eBook, then putting collectively an educational or informational e-book or better still, some type of eProduct inclusive of a DVD series, software, app, instructional CD set, online course, podcasts, technical video or anything that would assist people and solve any technical problems etc., this ought to now not be too difficult (specially as you could outsource in which wished). There is a large readymade customer base on Instagram, (now not which you must forestall the use of all of the different social media systems as well), for this form of product.

These products can be sold anywhere and there may be no interaction (until you need it). They regularly begin at several hundred bucks and may be up to date as wished or you can ask for an email cope with to ship them updates so these people become part of your email base. You need to be looking to upload to your e mail at every opportunity as it's far your first-class supply of high high-quality traffic. High nice within the sense that they've already bought from you so are very likely to achieve this again, without an excessive amount of persuasion, in particular when you have supplied good satisfactory for cash in the past.

Revenue Sharing

There are lots of folks who do no longer need to or can't be troubled with setting up their personal internet site and do no longer have a product to sell. This is in which a number of the revenue sharing sites can assist offer you with the opportunity to earn money online without having to do all this greater stuff and take some time to learn how.

If you desire to jot down for pleasure or as a hobby you can additionally make a few greater passive profits by means of writing high best articles and filing them to a variety of various locations on sales sharing websites.

Squidoo

Squidoo is a writing platform that lets you create pages with wealthy content material after which use those pages to sell products for income and plenty of humans use it to marketplace Amazon and eBay merchandise, however to earn whatever from commercials on Squidoo, they need to include a buying angle.

Hubpages

Hubpages is much like Squidoo; it's far a content material community for writers. Members have their own sub-domain, in which they put up their content material-wealthy articles (called Hubs). As a author for Hubpages (or Hubber), maximum of your earnings come from your very own Google AdSense account and sites together with Kontera, as well as eBay and Amazon Affiliate programs. They use sales splitting, which is accomplished by way of alternating the code utilized in advertisements: Your code will be displayed 60% of the time, and HubPages' code 40%. This website online is one of the 500 maximum visited US websites on the Internet.

Infobarrel

Infobarrel is a site this is smaller than Squidoo and Hubpages, but its income program lets in you to hold a majority of the money that your articles earn frequently as a publisher and you're entitled to 75% of the revenue generated from the show commercials to your articles. Infobarrel pays at once to writers, not like Squidoo and Hubpages, so all you need is a PayPal account which can be a bonus in case you are just beginning out. InfoBarrel boards have a regular thread entitled 'InfoBarrel Earnings Reports', making it smooth to look what different writers are earning.

Conclusion

Thank you for taking the time to read my e book, I hope it has given you some practical thoughts on some of the specific ways to move about constructing a passive profit for yourself over the long term. By taking a tough examine your personal state of affairs and seeing if there are any areas you may be capable of improve in your monetary situation, you're taking the primary steps to becoming independent. A passive profits, by means of definition, is in which you do a certain amount of labor to offer an asset that you may make a return on. Some human beings have real estate that they gather leases on or buy cheap and promote at a higher earnings, others make investments their cash in shares or bonds and live off the proceeds. For a few people that don't have the capital to make a massive funding with the intention to carrier a lifestyle they wish to have, they will want to use other options including developing or writing eBooks. This type of funding can pay off as the book has the capacity to keep promoting for lots years.

Usually the those who are a success at acquiring a long term passive income achieve this through careful making plans and spreading their resources over as huge a place as is plausible as this may reduce the probabilities of any losses and maximize the probabilities of gaining a higher income from your earnings base. The vintage saying 'don't keep all of your eggs in one basket' may be very wise. Many investors have come undone due to the fact they over invested in most effective one vicinity and had been not able to take in the losses they incurred.

Spending above your total capacity or now not contemplating the want to provider and preserve your internet presence as well as taking dangers that don't payoff are recipes for disaster and need to be avoided. But not unusual experience and forethought can pass a long way to preventing maximum problems. If you get benefit we hope to get your review on amazon kindle.

Sincerely

James Dollar

www.ingramcontent.com/pod-product-compliance
Lightning Source LLC
Chambersburg PA
CBHW080439220526
45465CB00009B/3344